All About America

WAGON TRAINS AND SETTLERS

Ellen H. Todras

KINGFISHER

NEW YORK

All About America: WAGON TRAINS AND SETTLERS
All rights reserved. No part of this book may be reproduced or utilized in any form or by any means, electronic or mechanical, including photocopying, recording, or by any information storage or retrieval systems, without permission in writing from the publisher.

KINGFISHER
LONDON & NEW YORK

Copyright © Bender Richardson White 2011

Published in the United States by Kingfisher,
175 Fifth Ave., New York, NY 10010
Kingfisher is an imprint of Macmillan Children's Books, London.
All rights reserved.

Distributed in the U.S. by Macmillan, 175 Fifth Ave.,
New York, NY 10010
Distributed in Canada by H.B. Fenn and Company Ltd.,
34 Nixon Road, Bolton, Ontario L7E 1W2

Library of Congress Cataloging-in-Publication data has been applied for.

ISBN paperback 978-0-7534-6511-0
ISBN reinforced library binding 978-0-7534-6583-7

Kingfisher books are available for special promotions and premiums. For details contact: Special Markets Department, Macmillan, 175 Fifth Ave., New York, NY 10010.

For more information, please visit www.kingfisherbooks.com

Printed in China
10 9 8 7 6 5 4 3 2 1
1TR/0311/WKT/UNTD/140MA

The All About America series was produced for Kingfisher by Bender Richardson White, Uxbridge, U.K.
Editor: Lionel Bender
Designer: Ben White
DTP: Neil Sutton
Production: Kim Richardson
Consultant: Richard Jensen, Research Professor of History, Culver Stockton College, Missouri

Sources of quotations and excerpts
Pages 4 and 16: Eaton, Herbert. *The Overland Trail to California in 1852.* New York: Putnam, 1974: pp.14, 67.
Pages 5, 19, 21, 28: Editors of Time-Life Books with text by Huston Horn. *The Settlers. [The Old West Series]* New York: Time-Life Books, 1974: pp. 26, 118, 200, 121.
Pages 6, 10, 14, 19, 24: Wadsworth, Ginger. *Words West: Voices of Young Settlers.* New York: Clarion, 2003: pp. 13, 39, 34, 90, 135, 137.
Page 25: from Wikimedia Commons:
http://commons.wikimedia.org/wiki/File:
Cherokee_Pass2.jpg

Acknowledgments
The publishers would like to thank the following illustrators for their contribution to this book: Mark Bergin, James Field, Inklink Firenze, John James, Peter Dennis, Gerald Wood. Map: Neil Sutton. Book cover design: Michael Yuen.

The publishers thank the following for supplying photos for this book: *b* = bottom, *c* = center, *l* = left, *t* = top, *m* = middle:
© The Art Archive: pages 24t (The Art Archive/Culver Pictures) • © Breslich & Foss: pages 8t; 8b; 12tr; 12br; 18t; 19b; 24ml; 27t •
© The Bridgeman Art Library: pages 4t and cover (Gift of F. Ethel Wickham in memory of W. Hull Wickham); 12–13 (Peter Newark American Pictures) • © Getty Images: pages 6 (Cincinnati Museum Center); 7 (Stock Montage); 11t (Transcendental Graphics); 12bl (Time & Life Pictures/Getty Images); 15t (English); 20tl (Jules Frazier); 21r (Superstock); 19t (Dorling Kindersley/Gary Ombler) • © istockphoto.com: pages 9br (Nikada); 10tl (stevecoleccs); 13tr (powerofforever); 14tl (jacomstephens); 14–15 (Anne de Haas); 20tl (Sydney Deem); 24m (Adam Mattel); 24b (Stephanie Howard); 26t (Alf Ertsland) •
© Library of Congress: pages 5tr (LC-DIG-ppmsca-03210); 16t (LC-USZ6-493); 25t (LC-DIG-ppmsc-04813); 28–29 (LC-DIG-pga-03320) • © www.shutterstock.com: pages 11mr and cover (donidotru); 13ml (pandapaw); 13bl (pandapaw) • © TopFoto.co.uk: AP/Topham pages 1, 2–3, 30–31, 32; The Granger Collection/TopFoto pages 1, 5tl, 6–7, 9, 10tr, 11ml 13mr, 14tr, 15b, 16m, 19m, 20b, 22bl, 23t, 23m, 27ml, 27mr, 28t, 29m; TopFoto/HIP pages 22–23, 23b.
Every effort has been made to trace the copyright holders of the images. The publishers apologize for any omissions.

Note to readers: The website addresses listed in this book are correct at the time of publishing. However, due to the ever-changing nature of the Internet, website addresses and content can change. Websites can contain links that are unsuitable for children. The publisher cannot be held responsible for changes in website addresses or content, or for information obtained through third-party websites. We strongly advise that Internet searches should be supervised by an adult.

CONTENTS

Introduction

Wagon Trains and Settlers looks at an important part of U.S. history from the early 1800s to around 1870. It focuses on why and how tens of thousands of people in eastern America moved west and set up homes in what are now the states of California, Oregon, Utah, and Washington. It explores the routes pioneers and settlers took, the wagons they traveled in, the hardships on the way, and the homes they built when they arrived. The story is presented as a series of double-page articles, each one looking at a particular topic. It is illustrated with paintings, engravings, and photographs from the time mixed with artists' impressions of everyday scenes and situations.

Beyond the Mississippi

Spreading west, opening up new lands

Following U.S. President Thomas Jefferson's Louisiana Purchase of 1803 and, later, the dream of Manifest Destiny, pioneers headed west. Most did so by wagon train. They created trails that led to Oregon and California.

"We started for that promised land on the thirteenth of April in . . . 1852," wrote Lewis Stout of Iowa. The promised land Stout was writing about was Oregon. His family was like thousands of other pioneers in the mid-1800s. They were looking for a better life out West.

Before Lewis and Clark's expedition of 1804 to 1806, most Americans knew almost nothing about the land beyond the Mississippi River. Interest in the West grew after Lewis and Clark returned. They brought back information about the plants, animals, and American Indians of the West. Fur traders and missionaries found routes to travel. Brave explorers and pioneers wrote handbooks on how to cross the plains, mountains, and deserts. In the 1840s, people began to move to Oregon and California.

Lewis and Clark

Meriwether Lewis and William Clark explored Louisiana Territory and Oregon Country. An American Indian woman, Sacagawea, helped them find their way. They gave Peace Medals to the chiefs they met.

▼ Settlers stopped at forts and trading posts along the trails. There they rested, fixed tools, and traded for supplies.

At forts, mountain men, settlers, and American Indians traded with one another, and settlers picked up information about conditions on the trail ahead.

Guidebook to the West

John C. Fremont was later called the Pathfinder, although he found no new paths. He explored the West in 1843 and 1844. Then he wrote a book about his travels, which many settlers used as a guide. In 1856, Fremont ran as the Republican candidate for president, but he was unsuccessful.

▲ This oil painting of 1872 is called *American Progress*. It shows the idea of Manifest Destiny as a beautiful woman leading the settlers west.

Manifest Destiny

A new idea called Manifest Destiny affected Americans' thinking. This was a belief that the United States was meant to stretch all the way to the Pacific Ocean. Wilson Morrison, a farmer from Missouri, said, "I allow the United States has the best right to that country, and I'm going to help make that right good."

▲ The major trails west across the United States

Mountain Men

Soon after Lewis and Clark explored the West, mountain men started living there. They trapped animals and sold their furs to trading companies. Mountain men such as Jim Bridger and Kit Carson found the paths that would become the routes the settlers followed. There were no paved roads—just wide paths that were packed with dirt in dry weather and deep with mud when it rained.

Why they came

First a trickle, then a stream, and then a flood of pioneers moved west. Many went to Oregon to farm the rich, free land. The gold rush of 1849 brought other people to California. They traveled thousands of miles on a trip that took about six months. Many of them went by wagon train, along with family, animals, and belongings. Their sense of adventure led them to new lands.

Westward Ho!
Following the pioneer trails

Lewis and Clark established routes west. Along the Missouri River in Missouri, settlers gathered to build wagons and to stock up for the journey west. They came from all parts of the East.

"In the spring of '46," Lucy Ann Henderson remembered, "my father . . . took me out of school, to my deep regret . . . My parents told me [we] were going to Oregon." In most families, fathers made this decision and then told their wives and children. Lucy Ann was sad, but some children were excited by the adventure.

Rivers were the highways of that time. You could travel from the Mississippi, Ohio, or Illinois rivers up the Missouri River. Many settlers took boats to St. Joseph or Independence. These towns were on the Missouri River. They were called jump-off points, and the overland routes began there.

Pressure for Land

This 1835 painting by John Caspar Wild is called *Cincinnati Public Landing*. It shows traffic by boat, horse, and foot at the port of Cincinnati on the Ohio River. People wanted the government to make land farther west open to them for farming and to build homes.

▶ Most wagon trails west started in Independence, Missouri.

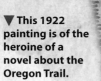
Immigrants and Emigrants

Immigrants are new people moving into an area; emigrants are those who leave their homes to live elsewhere. The picture, right, shows European Mormon immigrants. They gathered at Battery Park in New York City. Soon they would travel to Utah.

▲ American Indians watch as a family in a covered wagon passes by on the trail to Oregon.

The Whitman story

Marcus and Narcissa Whitman were Christian missionaries. They traveled west to convert American Indians to their religion. In 1836, they built a mission, Waiilatpu, among the Cayuse people. Waiilatpu is in what is now eastern Washington. The Whitmans helped new settlers arriving from the East. But tragedy struck in 1847. Many Cayuse people were dying of measles. The white people at Waiilatpu were not. The Cayuse believed that the white people did not try to save them, and they attacked and killed 14 white people. The Whitmans were among the dead.

The Wagons

Wooden homes on wheels

The wagons used for the trip west were called prairie schooners. A schooner is a type of sailing ship, and with the wagons' canvas-covered tops, a wagon train looked like a fleet of ships sailing one behind another across an ocean.

▶ An ox yoke

▼ Most families walked alongside the wagon. Wooden ox yokes kept the oxen in line as they drew the loaded wagon onward.

For a successful trip, the wagon had to be light enough for the oxen or mules to pull it, yet strong enough to last across 2,000 miles (3,200 km) of rough trails. Wagons were made of hard woods such as hickory, maple, or oak. The bed of the wagon was a rectangle, about 4 feet (1.2 m) wide by 10 feet (3 m) long. A frame of hickory bows supported a white canvas cover. The canvas was oiled to make it rainproof, and its sides could be tied up in hot weather. The wheels were made of hard wood, covered with flat iron tires. A bucket of grease, used to lubricate the wheels, hung under the wagon bed. The wagons had no brakes.

Guides and Routes

Starting in the 1830s, pioneers wrote guidebooks telling settlers how to make the overland journey west. Below is the title page of a guide to California published in 1852. There are handwritten notes opposite. Other books described the route to Oregon.

Those who can, walk

The wagon bed was filled with household goods and food for the trip. Any items taken on at the start of the journey that got in the way or weighed down the wagon too much were thrown out and left to rot on the trail. The only people who rode in the wagon were pregnant women, the sick, and the elderly. The wagon ride was not comfortable anyway. Wagons did not have springs, so riders bumped up and down on the uneven, unpaved trail. Most people preferred strolling beside the wagon to riding in it.

There were many rivers to cross on the trip. If the river was low, settlers just drove the wagons across, hitched to the mules or oxen. If the river was high, settlers floated the wagon beds across without the animals. This method was sometimes dangerous because a wagon bed could flip. But it usually worked.

In Times of Illness

A mother whose children were too young or too ill to walk rode in the wagon and tended to them. Conditions there were stifling. The cover trapped the heat of the sun—but it did keep out the dust and insects. Far from doctors, some people died on the trails. Children whose parents died were taken in by other families on the trail.

▶ Wagon wheels were made of wood with a metal rim around the edge.

▶ This Conestoga wagon pulled by horses was probably used to ship goods on the Santa Fe Trail to the Southwest. Conestoga, Pennsylvania, is where this type of wagon was first made.

Hitching Up
Animal-powered transportation

In the spring, settlers gathered at jump-off points on the Missouri River. They chose among horses, mules, and oxen to pull their wagons. They traveled in groups for safety, in long "trains" of wagons.

Nine-year old Catherine Sager remembered how her father "had two yoke of well-broken oxen; the rest were young and unbroken, and as he was not used to driving, he had much difficulty." The captain of the Sagers's wagon train had to teach Mr. Sager how to control his animals. The Sager family was not uncommon. Not only did animals often need to be taught to pull wagons, but the animals' owners also needed lessons in leading animals. Settlers spent long hours debating which animal was best to pull the wagons across the country. Most agreed that horses were not strong enough to last the trip. Mules were faster than oxen, but oxen cost less. They also fed on grass, while mules needed grain. Most settlers ended up with oxen as their "horsepower."

A bullwhip

Bullwhackers
Some wagon trains hired bullwhackers—men whose job it was to drive the oxen. Every bullwhacker had his bullwhip. Some whips were 20 feet (6 m) long. The oxen responded to the bullwhacker's commands: "gee" = turn right; "haw" = turn left; "whoa" = stop.

▶ Both horses and oxen pull the wagons in this wagon train. Notice the number of people walking and the bullwhacker beside the oxen.

▼ An illustration for historian Francis Parkman's 1847 book *The Oregon Trail*.

▲ This wagon train crossed the plains in 1869.

▶ This compass was used by settlers on the Santa Fe Trail.

A group journey

Many settlers traveled out west with their extended families. Brothers and their families, or grandparents, parents, and children often moved together. Several family groups might join up to make the trip as one wagon train. They often helped one another along the way. For example, the woman who made the first fire for evening dinner would share her fire with the other women who were cooking. There was, however, such a thing as too many wagons in one wagon train. The best number was between 20 and 30.

Wagon Captains

Before leaving its jump-off point, every wagon train elected officers and two captains as leaders. Some wagon trains had a pilot, too, who advised routes and chose campsites.

Rolling Along
Needs for a long journey

Settlers wanted to take as much as they could on the journey because tools and furniture would be rare and costly at their destination. Yet wagon loads needed to be as light as possible.

The most important thing to bring was food. During the winter and spring before they left for the West, families prepared dried fruit, hardtack, and salted meat for the trip. They packed eggs in barrels of flour and corn meal and brought coffee to drink because it hid the taste of the alkaline water on the plains. Some settlers took cows for both their meat and their milk. Families left extra milk in a pail beneath the wagon. By the end of a day on the bumpy trail, the milk was churned into butter.

▼ **Notice the spinning wheel, the kerosene lamp, and the fancy chair in this covered wagon.**

Schoolbooks
Most children were excited by the thought of no school for the six-month journey. Still, many parents brought schoolbooks along and taught their children as they traveled the trail. The children wrote and did their math problems with chalk on a slate.

Everything but the Kitchen Sink
Food took up most space in the wagon, but many settlers could not bear to leave behind treasured items such as a rocking chair or good dishes. They also brought blankets or quilts, clothing, and shoes for each family member.

▶ **Candles, a coffee grinder, and kitchen items**

12

Tools for a new life ahead

Settlers brought along the tools they would need to start a new life. Farmers brought plows, hoes, and rakes. Women brought needles, scissors, and other sewing items, for all sewing was done by hand until the 1860s. A cast-iron skillet on legs to cook in was a necessity. So were a water keg, a coffeepot and grinder, soap, and a tent. Many farmers brought along a spare yoke for oxen. If a yoke broke during the trip and the family did not have a replacement, they might have to leave the entire wagon behind.

◀ Some settlers used Dr. Thomas's Eclectic Oil to ease the pain of sore muscles.

◀ This schoolbook and magazine were published for American children around 160 years ago.

A family group of Mormons rest on the way to Utah in 1867.

Illness and Medicines

Settlers often bought medicine from a salesman—and it was completely useless. Some people made medicines from herbs growing nearby. People tried not to get sick; illness on the trail was often fatal.

▶ An 1878 colored engraving of settlers hunting on the trail

Hunting for Food

Every man in a wagon train had at least one rifle, hunting knife, and tomahawk. There were millions of buffalo on the plains, and settlers killed them for fresh meat and for their hides to turn into leather. They also hunted antelope, deer, rabbits, pheasants, and other wild animals.

▲ Settlers used hunting rifles such as these to kill animals for food.

Daily Routine

Round-the-clock

As the settlers began their long trip across the plains, desert, and mountains, life on the trail got into a routine. Men, women, and children had different duties on the trip.

Morning chores began at 4:00 A.M., long before sunrise. Within the corral, the circle of wagons, women built fires for cooking breakfast. Men rustled up the cattle and horses and gave them food and water. After breakfast, settlers took down the tents, loaded the wagons, and yoked the oxen. One group of young men set out for the morning to hunt buffalo or other game. A bugle blown at 7:00 A.M. started the wagons off on another day on the trail.

The wagon at the end of the train one day got to start the train the next day. The farther back in the train a wagon was, the dustier the ride. Some men rode on the front of their wagons, and some walked beside. Most women and children walked, 11 hours a day. Sometimes they picked flowers or herbs to eat along the trail. "We looked upon [the trip] as a great picnic," one teenager recalled.

▲ This bugle was used to mark important events in the daily routine.

Dogs on the Trail

Some people left their pets when they traveled west, and others brought their pets along. Some pets survived the journey, but most did not—they were killed by wild animals, died of hunger or disease, or just ran off. One dog named Tiger was fitted with leather boots by his 13-year-old owner to protect his paws on the trail.

▶ Families enjoyed dinnertime as a welcome change from the long hours of daily walking.

JEANIE WITH THE LIGHT B...

◀ "Jeanie with the Light Brown Hair," a song of the 1850s, was popular with the settlers.

Nooning and evening

At noon the bugle was blown again, signaling a break called nooning. Settlers enjoyed a light meal and a short rest before starting up again. The afternoons wore by slowly, everyone tiring of the journey. The pilot rode off in advance of the wagons to find a good place to stop for the night.

As the sun dipped down in the sky, the train stopped for the night. Children found buffalo chips to fuel fires. Men tended the animals and set up tents. Women cooked dinner, usually bacon and bread, or fresh meat if the hunters had been successful. If the family owned cows, they would enjoy milk and butter with their meal. They sat on blankets as they ate. In the evenings, when settlers were not too tired, families gathered as someone told stories or played tunes on a flute or fiddle. Children helped their mothers make dough, leaving it to rise to make bread, biscuits, and muffins the next breakfast-time.

▲ Settlers danced a square dance to celebrate a special event, mark their progress on the trail, or relieve boredom.

Circling the Wagons

Settlers camped at night with their wagons in a circle for protection for themselves and their animals.

Forts and Supplies
A chance to restock and exchange news

Scattered along the Oregon Trail were several forts and trading posts. Other staging posts developed along the California and Mormon trails. A postal service sprang up to allow communication with loved ones far away.

▲ **Madeline of Fort Reno**, a popular play in the 1800s, took place at a fort in the West.

After long weeks on the trail and not seeing any other people, arriving at a fort or trading post was a welcome change for settlers. The first stop, Fort Kearny in Nebraska, was built in 1848 to protect emigrants. By the time settlers reached the next stop, Fort Laramie in present-day Wyoming, they had completed about one-third of their journey. They were now near the Rocky Mountains.

Beyond the Rockies

Fort Bridger, pictured here in 1852, was on the western side of the Rocky Mountains. The fort was built by mountain man Jim Bridger after the fur trade faded.

▲ This busy fort, located west of the Rocky Mountains, was built of wood. Men in the watchtower looked out for attacks by American Indians.

At the Store

Settlers stopped at forts to get needed supplies. Here, a mother and daughter look at material while a father and son test a rifle. Purchases, if wrapped at all, were wrapped in old newspaper. At a fort, a family might also get a good meal. One settler wrote, "Procured here a good meal of bread, fresh butter, and milk, and ate so much that it gave me a violent headache and made me quite sick all night."

To California or Utah

At Fort Hall in present-day Idaho, the Oregon Trail split. Settlers headed for California turned south, traveling through harsh desert and the Sierra Nevada before reaching Sutter's Fort in California. This is where the gold rush of 1849 began.

The Mormons (see page 23) began to emigrate to Utah in 1847. They traveled on the northern side of the Platte River, avoiding other settlers who used the southern side. They set up guideposts every 10 miles (16 km) for those who followed them. Thousands of Mormons waited in encampments until getting the okay to move on.

▼ Plains Indians set up tepees outside Fort Laramie and traded with settlers.

▲ Trading posts carried supplies to help settlers complete their journey.

Trading at Fort Laramie

Unlike most forts, Fort Laramie was built of adobe—bricks that are dried in the sun. It was first a trading post but was bought by the U.S. Army in 1849 as a military camp. Plains Indians came to trade at Fort Laramie. They brought horses, meat, moccasins, and fresh vegetables for emigrants who passed through. Emigrants traded rifles, blankets, whiskey, and knives for their supplies.

Sending mail—settler style

Early settlers used simple methods to send and receive mail. People sent letters home with those returning to the East. A settler's daughter named Virginia Reed wrote about "prairic post offices," where letters were pinned to sticks at popular campsites. One traveler said he passed a barrel marked "Post Office" beside the trail. In time, as settlements sprang up along the trail, mail was exchanged in a more organized way. Forts and trading posts had U.S. post offices within them.

Mishaps and Dangers
Traveling into the unknown

There was another side to the adventures settlers had on the trail. They faced hardships and hazards that they had never before experienced. Some settlers did not reach the end of the trail.

Before leaving on their journey, many settlers imagined that the greatest danger would be American Indians. Instead it was illness, which was also the greatest cause of death. People did not know about the benefits of cleanliness and a good diet. Often no doctor was available, and the medicines were not as effective as those of today.

Settlers also had to avoid buffalo stampedes and getting run over by wagons. Snake bites and insect bites could become infected. A good number of adults and children drowned while crossing rivers. Drinking bad water could kill a person, too. Sometimes children wandered off and got lost on the plains.

Extremes of Weather

Settlers experienced extremes of weather on their way west. Crossing a blazing desert in August or September sapped the strength of even the hardiest settlers. Below, a family is struggling through a snowstorm, which often happened in the mountains toward the end of the trip.

▲ This medicine chest belonged to a settler family. People often brought quinine for malaria, peppermint for stomach illness, and castor oil and rum to help digestion.

▲ Children huddled to keep warm as adults pushed wagons through the snow. Sometimes wagons were abandoned so that people could save their lives.

18

Death on the trail

One out of every 17 settlers who started on the Oregon Trail was buried there. Most were killed by disease, especially cholera. The cholera germ was carried up the Mississippi River from New Orleans, and settlers spread it westward. Usually, when someone came down with cholera, the wagon train stopped and waited for the person to die. People buried their loved ones quickly and moved on. Travelers often passed graves every 100 yards (90 m). As Eliza Ann McCauley reached the Rockies, she wrote, "Here we saw the graves of two sisters, acquaintances of ours, on their way to Oregon."

Describing the Dangers

Today we know about the dangers of the journeys because of the words settlers left behind. In the journal below, the page on the left is part of a daily description; the page on the right is a figuring of miles traveled on the trail.

▼ Here, a group of settlers come upon a broken wagon with no surviving people or animals.

▶ ▼ Pages of an Oregon Trail journal

Awful stories

Sometimes something terrible happened to a wagon train. In 1845, hundreds of emigrants took an unexplored cutoff in eastern Oregon to save time. Instead they got lost in the mountains. At least 23 people died. Even worse was the Donner Party story of 1846. A group of 81 people traveling to California left late and tried to make up time by taking a shortcut. They were stranded in the Sierra Nevada for months. By the time they were rescued, 34 people had died. Virginia Reed, one of the survivors, later wrote to a cousin back home, "Never take no cutoffs and hurry along as fast as you can."

Encounters with Indians

Meetings of two cultures end in clashes

When settlers crossed the North American continent, they often met groups of the first native peoples—American Indians. The ancestors of these groups had lived on the land for thousands of years. Everything was about to change.

At first, the pioneers were only crossing the plains, not settling on them. American Indians often helped them continue westward. Both groups were curious about each other. Some American Indian warriors enjoyed examining the contents of the wagons. Usually, American Indians wanted to trade goods, such as fresh food for rifles, mirrors, or sewing needles.

▶ **American Indian arrows**

▲ **An American Indian shield may have protected against arrows but not rifle bullets.**

Raid on the Plains

In general, American Indians did not attack wagon trains. Until white men sold them guns, they had only bows and arrows as weapons. Sometimes they would steal horses from the corral, however. Mostly they attacked only single wagons crossing the plains.

Frederic Remington painted this picture, *The Emigrants,* many years after the last wagon train crossed the country.

Confrontations and terror

As wagon trains got larger and people settled on the plains, conflicts began. Settlers killed the buffalo that Plains Indians needed for food and shelter. Settlers' cattle and oxen ate the grass that Plains Indians' horses needed for food. Tensions began to rise. As attacks on settlers increased, the government took over trading posts and built military forts to house soldiers who fought American Indians. When gold was discovered, as happened in South Dakota in 1874, soldiers forced American Indians onto reservations, even though the government had promised that this would not happen. On reservations, the American Indians found it almost impossible to live as they had previously and to maintain their customs.

► A settler mother protects her children as the father confronts approaching Sioux Indians.

▼ In this 1856 painting, pioneers use rifles against the American Indians' tomahawks and bows and arrows.

The Homestead Act of 1862

The Homestead Act opened government land in the West to settlers. The American Indians who lived there were forced out and many were killed by diseases and in massacres. In 1870, Red Cloud, a Sioux chief, visited President Ulysses S. Grant in Washington, D.C. His words capture American Indians' deep disappointment with their situation: "When we first had this land we were strong. Now we are melting like snow on the hillside, while you are growing like spring grass." By 1900, only about 200,000 American Indians lived in the United States, most of them on reservations.

◄ American Indian warriors sometimes formed "war parties" and attacked pioneers and settlers.

The Major Trails
Routes across country

The Oregon Trail was the main route westward, but wagon trains were used on other journeys as well. Main routes included the California Trail, the Mormon Trail, and the Santa Fe Trail.

▼ As this wagon train crosses a river on the California Trail, settlers dump water from their boots.

▲ Crossing rivers was physically exhausting. Some people drowned.

Sutter's Fort

At the time settlers began to head west, Mexico owned California. A Swiss man, John Sutter, convinced the Mexican government to grant him a huge piece of land in northern California. He built a fort there and became a rich landowner. In 1848, he built a sawmill on the American River. While walking along the river, the head carpenter saw yellow flecks in the water—and started a gold rush. John Sutter was well known for helping pioneers and selling land to settlers.

▲ Sutter's Fort became the endpoint of the California Trail.

Going for the gold

Most of the people who went to California soon after 1848 hoped to make their fortunes in gold, rather than farm the land. Most were men who planned to return home wealthy in a short time. Some went by sea, sailing around the tip of South America. But the majority went across the continent in wagon trains.

After settlers crossed South Pass in the Rockies, the California Trail broke off from the Oregon Trail. From there, settlers had some options. If they took Sublette's Cutoff, the way was shorter but there was no water. They could also go to Fort Bridger, where supplies were available. Finally, after the Mormons settled in Salt Lake City, a third option was available. If settlers needed to fix their wagon or get fresh oxen, they might choose the route through Salt Lake City.

An unlikely paradise

In 1847, the first group of Mormons left the eastern United States in search of religious freedom. They were by far the most organized group to cross the plains and mountains. A small group worked in advance of the main group, smoothing the trail and creating way stations for rest, shelter, and food. Their conversations with several mountain men convinced them that the valley south of the Great Salt Lake was to be their new home. When they reached this valley, people said, "This is the place." Within weeks, they had planted crops for the thousands of Mormons to follow them.

Mormons traveled from Illinois to Utah in 1847.

The Santa Fe Trail
This trail was the earliest way used by wagon trains in the West. It opened in 1820 and stretched from the town of Independence, Missouri, to Santa Fe, New Mexico. Later, trails were made to Los Angeles and San Diego, California.

The State of Deseret
The Mormons formed the State of Deseret in present-day Utah. It existed until 1851. The state produced its own banknotes. This one (above) was issued at Salt Lake City. It was used by farmers to buy livestock.

◀ **Mormon Brigham Young led the group to their home in the desert.**

Over Desert and Mountain

To reach the Pacific was still a long, hard trek

Once past the Great Plains, there were natural barriers that had to be crossed. The first, the Rocky Mountains, were easy by comparison, with South Pass leading through the peaks. The deserts that followed were the greatest challenges of all.

By the time settlers prepared to cross desert land, they had been traveling for months. Before crossing, they filled all possible containers with water, including shoes and pots. Some cut grass and stored it for food for their animals. But the deserts showed no mercy. People crossing the Forty-Mile-Desert on the California Trail noted hundreds of dead animals beside the trail. Fourteen-year-old Sallie Hester, who crossed a desert farther north on the Oregon Trail in 1849, wrote: "The weary journey last night . . . with the cry of 'Another ox down,' the stopping of the train to unyoke the poor dying brute . . . and the weary, weary tramp of men and beasts worn out with heat and famished for water, will never be erased from my memory."

▲ Journeying over mountains, wagon trains traveled around 1.5 miles (2.4 km) a day.

Doing the impossible

After deserts, there were more mountains—the Wasatch Mountains and the Sierra Nevada on the California Trail and the Blue Mountains on the Oregon Trail. Cutting through the Wasatch Mountains, the Donner Party (see page 19) had to move huge boulders and cut heavy brush. Sometimes they lifted or lowered wagons one by one over steep riverbanks. Train leader Jesse Applegate recorded crossing the Blue Mountains in a snowstorm, "wading through mud and snow and suffering from the cold and wet."

▶ Settlers carried the tools of their trades and used these mallets, chisels, and wood planers to repair wagons.

Carving Names

Sometimes settlers passed a place where it was easy to carve into the rock. At Independence Rock, just east of South Pass on the Sweetwater River, settlers might stop to carve their names and a date as a record of their trek. Some names are still visible today on what remain of the trails.

Crossing the Great Rockies

The Rocky Mountains, up to 14,000 feet (4,270 m) high and many miles wide, were formidable. Daniel Jenks drew this picture (right) of Cherokee Pass in the Rockies. He was part of a wagon train that struggled through here on June 7, 1859. Jenks noted that when they stopped for the day, "our wagons had to be chained to keep them in their places, the hillside was so steep." Jenks finally returned to his home in Rhode Island.

▶ A mother with a young baby to feed would have found the desert and mountain journey particularly hard.

▶ This family has had to stop to fix a broken spoke in a wheel of their wagon. They have to work hard so they can catch up to their wagon train once the wagon is repaired.

The Journey's End

Staking claims and settling down

Most settlers on the Oregon Trail ended up as farmers in the Willamette Valley of Oregon. Many of those on the California Trail became miners in the gold rush. Mormons followed their trail to new homes in Utah. Some settlers set up homes at points along each trail.

▼ An ax used to chop down trees

In Oregon, settlers endured much hard work building a new life. They first chose a good home site. As more people arrived, finding one became more challenging. Next, settlers built their homes, even if they arrived in the cold of winter. They lived in their wagons until the walls and roofs were up. Neighbors helped in cabin-raisings, but the owner spent weeks getting the logs ready. The families also had to plant seeds for food. They went hungry until fields yielded food.

▼ Every family member, even the children, helped on the homestead.

▶ The wagon was sometimes used as a spare room or for carrying goods.

Staking a claim

The thirst for gold lured thousands of people to California, but they were not interested in homesteads. Instead, they wanted to stake a claim on land to mine for gold. They were called the forty-niners because so many of them rushed to California in 1849, soon after gold was discovered. There was no government to oversee land ownership, so they made their own rules. It was truly the Wild West.

▼ A horse pulls a settler's plow through cleared land.

A group of miners formed a district when a gold deposit was found in an area. Each miner could have one claim, except the discoverer of the deposit, who got two claims. Claims were as small as 10 square feet (1 sq m) at first because the deposits were so rich. Nonwhites and people from other countries could not make a claim, but slavery was not allowed.

California's population boomed. Between 60,000 and 100,000 people streamed to California in 1849. Some went home penniless without having found gold, but others kept coming. By 1853, more than 220,000 people lived in California.

▼ Exodusters board riverboats for St. Louis.

Clearing Land for Crops

Unlike the Great Plains that most settlers crossed to come west, Oregon had huge evergreen forests. Settlers needed to clear their land in order to grow crops. First, they chopped down the trees, using the wood for their homes. Many farmers had to plow by hand, which was back-breaking work that took weeks to complete. Those who had a horse used the animal to pull the plow, making the work much easier and quicker.

The Exodusters

After the Civil War ended in 1865, some African Americans in the South felt threatened by the white population. In 1879 and 1880, thousands of them migrated west to Kansas and homesteaded there. Many sailed from Vicksburg, Mississippi, to St. Louis, then went by wagon, rail, or on foot. These migrants were called the Exodusters, after the Exodus in the Bible.

Settling in the West

From villages to towns to cities

Where the trails ended, villages sprang up. Instead of farming or mining, some settlers stayed in towns and built new lives there. Some towns of the western United States grew into cities.

▲ This 1923 poster advertised the silent movie *The Covered Wagon,* one of the first movies about the West.

The Oregon Trail ended at Oregon City, on the Willamette River. Settlers had few possessions by the time they arrived in Oregon. In 1844, there were three stores in Oregon City. Since there was little or no money, settlers turned to barter, or trade by exchange, for the things they needed. Farms were far apart, and settlers welcomed opportunities to meet and socialize. At church, they not only worshiped but also discussed the latest news, crop prices, and even gossip. One settler with a sense of humor wrote: "I never saw so fine a population as in Oregon. They were honest, because there was nothing to steal; sober, because there was no liquor; there were no misers because there was no money; they were industrious, because it was work or starve."

Town in the Wilderness

In early Oregon City, stagecoaches provided transportation for passengers, and freight wagons carried goods. Beyond the houses were farms, where settlers grew crops to feed the town. In the distance was the forest from which the town was cut. Oregon City had the first newspaper, mail delivery, jail, and library west of the Rockies. From 1844 to 1852 it served as Oregon Territory's capital.

▼ Settlers enjoyed themselves at county fairs, including pig wrestling!

Governments and statehood

Settlers also felt the need for government to make laws and resolve conflicts. In 1843, Oregon settlers wrote a constitution and a bill of rights. Slavery was outlawed. Every man could claim 1 square mile (2.6 sq km) of land. Oregon became a state in 1859. In California, lawlessness plagued San Francisco in 1849. Hundreds of ships, abandoned by people seeking gold, clogged the harbor. Trash was not collected; water was unsafe to drink; and murderers went uncaught. As part of the effort to resolve these problems, California became a state in 1850.

After the transcontinental railroad was completed in 1869, traveling overland by wagon became less and less popular. By 1890, settlers had claimed most of the good land out West. Wagon trains passed into history, but the stories of these brave settlers live on.

A riverside view of Oregon City, as painted in 1848

Portland Near the Pacific

The picture below shows the town of Portland, Oregon, in about 1885. The town grew up on the banks of the Willamette River and the Columbia River, which leads to the Pacific Ocean. By this time it had become an important port on the West Coast. By 1890, Portland had a population of 18,000.

Glossary

adobe bricks that are dried in the sun

alkaline containing bitter mineral salts

buffalo chips clumps of buffalo dung

bullwhacker person who drove a wagon on the wagon trail

cholera disease of the intestines, often ending in death

corral circle of wagons

emigrant person who leaves his or her home to live elsewhere

expedition journey made for a purpose such as exploring the land

gold rush starting in 1849, the time when people went to California to try to find gold

hardtack hard crackers made of flour and water

immigrant person who once lived elsewhere and moves to a new place

jump-off point place where the journey west began for many wagon trains

Louisiana Purchase huge tract of land west of the Mississippi River purchased from France in 1803

Manifest Destiny the idea that the United States was meant to stretch all the way west to the Pacific Ocean. *Manifest* means "easy to see or understand," and *destiny* means "something that is meant to be."

missionaries people who try to convert others to their religion

mountain men traders and fur trappers who lived in the Rocky Mountains mainly between the 1820s and 1840s. Their knowledge of the West was a great help to settlers.

mule work animal that is the result of mating a male donkey and female horse

oxen cattle raised to do work; usually adult males

pilot person in a wagon train who advised routes and chose campsites

pioneer person who does something first for others, such as settlers, to follow

plains wide area of flat or gently rolling land. The Great Plains is land between the Mississippi River and the Rocky Mountains.

prairie large area of grassy land with few or no trees

Republican Party political party that began in the 1850s on an antislavery platform

reservation area of land set aside by the government for American Indians to live on

Rocky Mountains main mountain system in the western United States; also known as the Rockies

settler someone new who comes to an area and sets up home

stampede sudden rush of a herd of animals such as buffalo

tepee cone-shaped tent used by Plains Indians

territory system of government used before there were enough people to form a state

transcontinental railroad railroad that connected the eastern and western parts of the United States

wagon train group of wagons traveling west together. A long line of wagons looked like the cars of a train or a line of sailing ships

yoke wooden frame used to join two animals such as oxen

Timeline

1792 American Robert Gray explores the Columbia River

1803 In the Louisiana Purchase, the United States buys central North America from France

1804–1806 The Lewis and Clark Expedition explores the West

1811 Oregon's first permanent settlement is started as a fur-trading post at Astoria, Oregon

1820 The Santa Fe Trail is opened

1835–1839 U.S. government forces American Indians to move to Indian Territory

1836 The Whitman Mission is set up in present-day Walla Walla, Washington

1841 The first organized wagon trains head for Oregon and California

1846 The United States and Britain set the present boundary between the United States and Canada

1846 The Donner Party tragedy takes place. Some reportedly eat the flesh of dead fellow emigrants (cannibalism) to stay alive

1847 The Cayuse Indians attack the Whitman Mission

1847 Brigham Young leads the first Mormons to Utah

1848 The United States pays $15 million to Mexico for California, Nevada, and Utah, and parts of Arizona, New Mexico, Colorado, and Wyoming

1849 California Gold Rush begins

1850 California becomes a state

1851 Utah becomes a territory

1853 Oregon Territory is divided into Oregon and Washington (which includes Idaho)

1853 In the Gadsden Purchase, the United States buys southwestern New Mexico and southern Arizona from Mexico

1859 Oregon becomes a state

1861–1865 The Civil War is fought

1862 Homestead Act is passed

1863 Idaho Territory is separated from Washington Territory

1869 Transcontinental railroad is completed

1879 Exodusters begin to arrive in Kansas

1889 Washington becomes a state

1890 Idaho becomes a state

Information

WEBSITES

End of the Oregon Trail Interpretive Center
www.historicoregoncity.org/HOC/
On the home page, click "History Resources"

The Oregon Trail: website for the PBS mini-series
www.isu.edu/~trinmich/Oregontrail.html

Covered Wagons of the Oregon Trail
www.highlightskids.com/Stories/NonFiction/ NF0597_coveredwagons.asp

California National Historic Trail
www.nps.gov/cali/index.htm

Historic Development of the California Trail
www.emigranttrailswest.org/caltrail.htm

The Mormon Settler Trail
www.lds.org/gospellibrary/pioneer/01_Convert _Immigrants.html

The Santa Fe Trail
www.santafetrail.org/index.php

BOOKS TO READ

Frazier, Neta Lohnes. *The Stout-Hearted Seven: Orphaned on the Oregon Trail*. New York: Sterling Point Books, 2006 (Updated Ed edition).

Hermes, Patricia. *Westward to Home: Joshua's Oregon Trail Diary*. New York: Scholastic, 2002.

Landau, Elaine. *The Oregon Trail*. New York: Children's Press (Scholastic), 2006.

Moss, Marissa. *Rachel's Journal: The Story of a Pioneer Girl*. San Diego, CA: Harcourt, 2001.

Thompson, Gare. *Our Journey West: The Oregon Trail Adventures of Sarah Marshall*. Washington, DC: National Geographic Society, 2003.

Wadsworth, Ginger. *Words West: Voices of Young Pioneers*. New York: Clarion, 2003.

Index